Dear Jesus... Love Sandy

Dear Jesus... Love Sandy

Sandra Drescher

ZONDERVAN
PUBLISHING HOUSE

OF THE ZONDERVAN CORPORATION | GRAND RAPIDS, MICHIGAN 49506

DEAR JESUS... LOVE SANDY
Copyright © 1982 by The Zondervan Corporation
Grand Rapids, Michigan

Third printing May 1982

Library of Congress Cataloging in Publication Data

Drescher, Sandra.
    Dear Jesus, love Sandy.

    I. Youth—Religious life. I. Title.
BV4531.2.D73   248'.8   81-23997
ISBN 0-310-44840-9
ISBN 0-310-44841-7 (pbk.)

All Scripture quotations are from the New International
Version, copyright 1978 by the New York International Bible
Society.

Edited by John Iwema
Designed by Louise Bauer

Printed in the United States of America

*To Rose
my lovely and loving sister,
who has influenced me greatly
in the beauty of her friendship
with Jesus*

Contents

Preface

A lot has happened in my life since my first book, *Just Between God and Me,* was published. College years, living on my own, working in several prisons, a number of bicycle trips in the U.S. and Canada, and, more recently, seminary training and working with juvenile offenders, to name just a few.

In the midst of all these new experiences, I've always held on tightly to one goal: growing closer to God. And I know that to do this, I have to talk to God about what's happening in my life.

Several years ago, I realized that my daily prayers were becoming routine. I often found my mind wandering as I talked to God, or I'd become distracted by someone or something and never finish. At nighttime, I'd sometimes fall asleep before I'd even finished praying!

Whenever I thought about Jesus as my Friend—the personal Friend I believed Him to be—I felt embarrassed. No friend deserves to be treated as rudely as I'd been

9

treating Him. I knew that my communication with God had to be revitalized; so I decided to begin writing my prayers.

Writing to Jesus (just like writing any letter) takes more time than talking to Him; but for me, it's been very helpful. Writing demands my attention, and it gives me a chance to sort out my thoughts. It's also a good reminder that Jesus really is listening. He wants to share my confusion, my joy, my sorrow—whatever I'm feeling.

When I first began, my written prayers were full of proper "God words." I thought Jesus was beyond my reach. I couldn't talk to Him in ordinary, everyday language.

It soon struck me that I wasn't hiding anything with this formality. Jesus knew all my thoughts and feelings. Talking to Him honestly and simply, just as I would to any other friend, was refreshing. It was also good to know the assurance of His constant love and acceptance as I admitted my deepest self to Him.

I'll always want to reverence God for His awesome majesty, but I also wish to share with you my readers the personal Friend I've found in Jesus. My hope is that you, too, will know the freedom of being honest with God. That's the reason for the blank page at the close of each of the prayers in this book. I hope that you'll use these pages to write out your prayers to Jesus, or perhaps to jot down joys and concerns—as well as praise!—that you'd like to tell Jesus about in your spoken prayers.

I'd like to make three suggestions about writing prayers. First, write about one thing rather than about many things. For example, tell Jesus about *one* of your needs or about *one* thing you're thankful for. In this way you'll be writing a prayer *journal* rather than a diary. Second, be sure to tell Jesus about your feelings—joy, sorrow, hope, fear, and many more—as well as your thoughts. Finally, as much as you can, do this writing at the same time each day. If you do, writing prayers has a much better chance of becoming part of your daily routine.

This book isn't the end of writing prayers for me. I continue to do this, and I don't see the end in sight! For me, written prayers are a few of the steps along the way in growing closer to God.

My prayer is that each person who reads these prayers will find inspiration to cultivate an honest, personal friendship with Jesus. I'm convinced this is the kind of relationship He wants to have with us.

Part One

I Lift My Eyes

Snow Jokes and Springtime

For the LORD is the great God, the great King above all gods. In his hand are the depths of the earth, and the mountain peaks belong to him. The sea is his, for he made it, and his hands formed the dry land.

Psalm 95:3–5

Dear Jesus,

Here it is the middle of spring and we're having a snowstorm! After a week of warm weather, it's a wonderful joke on us. I love it and I love You for sending it. Every time You cover the ground with a new blanket of white, it reminds me how much You love fun.

An unexpected snowfall is especially exciting. So are the first buds in spring, the first bumblebee in the summer, and the first leaves turning color in fall. Once a new season has arrived, though, it's too easy to take the beauty for granted. Why is that, Lord? Green grass is just as amazing and just as wonderful when summer is half over as at the beginning. Thunderstorms are always awesome (and scary!), not just the first few in the spring.

I remember my first canoe trip in Canada. Most of my friends had been there before, and they got tired of my oohs and ahs! But when my friends from Illinois visit me, they talk much more about the moun-

15

tains of Virginia than I do. Of course it's because I've lived near these mountains for six years.

That seems so ironic, Jesus—almost sinful! Maybe I should schedule specific times each week, or every day, to thank You for your creation. You've made it for me to enjoy. Help me make praise so much a part of me that it's as natural as breathing. You deserve it, Jesus, even though I don't always act like I believe that. I get so bogged down by "important" details of living that I almost forget life's real meaning.

Open my eyes to the beauty of what too often becomes ordinary, Jesus. Help me to laugh with children, to stop and smell the flowers, to kick my shoes off and squish the mud between my toes, to look for animal figures in the clouds. And remind me that I can only enjoy them because You make it possible.

In praise and thanksgiving,
Sandy

*Were there no God, we would be in this
glorious world with grateful hearts; and no
one to thank.*

CHRISTINA GEORGINA ROSSETTI

(This page is for the reader to write her or his prayers.)

17

Learning to Listen

Listen, listen to me, and eat what is good, and your soul will delight in the richest of fare. Give ear and come to me; hear me, that your soul may live.

Isaiah 55:2–3

Dear Jesus,

I was just thinking about how much time I spend talking to You—out loud, in my thoughts, in writing, and with others. But how much time do I spend listening to You? The more I think, the worse I feel, because I realize that I haven't been a very good listener.

What started me thinking was a story Marge told me last week. It was about a little boy whose parents bought him a toy telephone. They wanted him to have something to play with on a long trip they were about to take. On the trip, he called everyone he knew and held imaginary conversations.

Finally he called You, Jesus. The striking thing was that after he talked, he waited while You talked. Then he responded to what he imagined You were saying. It's a bit embarrassing to admit how profound that seems to me. You said, "The kingdom of heaven belongs to such as these" (Matt.

19

19:14). You sure used this story to show me another corner of Your kingdom!

Since I heard that I've been thinking about how often I call you and then don't bother to wait for Your response. Even when I'm asking You for advice or direction! I love writing my prayers to You. It always helps me a lot. But if it's a monologue, I'm only being half blessed, and our fellowship is never complete. Why is it that I'm content with doing all the communicating during *our* trips together?

I know I need to spend a lot more time listening to You, Jesus. Help me to do that. Help me to clear other thoughts from my mind and allow our conversations to be dialogues.

As a starter, I'm going to stop writing and start listening right now.

Silenced,
Sandy

How can you expect God to speak in that gentle inward voice which melts the soul when you are making so much noise with your rapid reflections? Be silent and God will speak again.

FRANCOIS FENELON

When We Call You Father

This is how you should pray: "Our Father in heaven...."

Matthew 6:9

Dear Jesus,

Writing my prayers to You is a real comfort to me. This morning I realized, again, the effect it's having on my whole life—what I say, what I do, how I think. When I think of You as a friend who always loves me, I can't help but want to be that kind of friend to You too.

I don't want to sound judgmental of other people, Jesus; but when we started saying Your prayer in church this morning, I just couldn't say it with everyone else. I got stuck after the first line.

I know that it wouldn't have been good if everyone in church had stopped praying, but now that we're alone, I need to talk more about it with You. When I think about how often I hurry through Your prayer without really thinking about the words, and multiply this by the number of others who probably do the same thing, I wonder if You ever wish You hadn't taught this prayer to Your disciples. Jesus, help us to realize the power in

23

the words and to say them with sincerity.

As we all began praying this morning, I felt a surge of unity with everyone who prays "Our Father"—both in our church and all over the world. This always makes me sure once again that God is my Father. I suddenly felt privileged beyond words to come to You as a sinner—to come to the One who is over everyone and everything!

I pledged to You my dependence and my complete trust. I know You love me and want the best for me. I want everything I do and think to be worthy of You.

Jesus, I know I've only begun to understand what I've recited for so long. Help me to be increasingly aware of the words I speak and also of the meaning they hold for our life together.

Yours forever,
Sandy

When thou prayest, rather let thy heart be
without words than thy words without heart.

JOHN BUNYAN

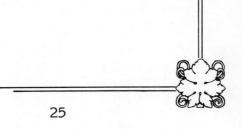

25

Of Mountains and Molehills

I will instruct you and teach you in the way you should go; I will counsel you and watch over you.

Psalm 32:8

Dear Jesus,

Sometimes I make mountains out of molehills. But since You talked about our faith moving mountains, You're the best One to talk to about the mountain I've created. It's time to make some more decisions about my future, and, true to form, I've procrastinated. So now I feel a lot of pressure.

To be honest, Jesus, my main problem is trying to figure out what You want me to do. How can I best be used by You? At this point, I think if I was absolutely sure of Your will, I'd be able to do anything. Sometimes I wish You'd bop me over the head and point me in the right direction. Or send a bird with a note from You. Then I'd know just what to do, and there'd be no more questions.

I hear people say, "The Lord told me . . ." and "The Lord said to . . ." Frankly, Jesus, I don't understand that. It seems like this kind of decision is such a long agonizing process for me. Does that mean I'm not really listening to You? Or does it perhaps

27

mean I can choose one of several possible directions and still be in Your will?

And isn't all this part of our Christian freedom? You've set clear moral bounds, and this limits my options. But you also give me some freedom to determine where my interests are leading me. This sounds good even as I'm writing it!

If I'm shying away from making a decision, I can't blame You for a discouraging day. That's what keeps me from being a robot! It's comforting, too, to know that whatever I decide to do, You'll be with me.

I've been able to narrow my choices by knowing what my values allow me to do and what my interests encourage me to do. This gives me some direction. Now it seems that I should hear from others, people who know me—and You!—well.

After all this, if I have inner peace about the direction that's emerging, I'll go ahead and commit myself to that course.

Talking with You about this is loosening the knots of anxiety already, Jesus. But it's still risky! I have one last request. If I make the wrong choice, please slam the door on me—hard.

Moving along,
Sandy

The will of God will not lead you where the grace of God cannot keep you.

ANONYMOUS

Depending On Independence

*I will praise you, O LORD, with all my
heart. . . . You made me bold and stouthearted.*
                              Psalm 138:1, 3

Dear Jesus,

I've been thinking a lot recently about
independence and about how it relates to
dependence on You and living in inter-
dependence on my spiritual brothers
and sisters. Society seems to say that
independence is the epitome of true
happiness. Or at least the goal of a mature
adult.

We're taught to strive for self-sufficiency
from childhood. As we become older, those
who demonstrate independence first and/or
most successfully get respect. I guess that's
not all bad. I'm glad I learned to walk and to
do things on my own. But where does it
stop? *Should* it stop, Jesus?

Am I confessing to a sin when I admit
that I own a bicycle and a car, and that I've
just made plans for the next fifteen months
of my life—consulting hardly anyone?
I know I've talked to You about each of these
decisions, and maybe these examples aren't
so bad in themselves. But they symbolize a

31

trend, and I'm not sure I've chosen this course.

When I compare my lifestyle with the one You chose for Your ministry—not even having a place of Your own to sleep—and with the way the early Christians lived—sharing all they had—I wonder how far away from that I can move and still be in Your will.

I know independence can be good, but I also see how easily it can become self-centeredness. I don't seek traveling companions as much as I used to, now that I have my own transportation. When I make decisions too much on my own, I often don't show people I need them—or remind myself how much I need others! When I live alone, I grow accustomed to my way of doing things. This can mean losing the gifts of flexibility and patience You've given me.

Thank You for pricking my conscience, Jesus, and getting me to think about the potential evils of independence. Keep me struggling to find a good balance between independence, dependence, and inter-dependence.

Depending on You,
Sandy

32

It is well for us to think that no grace or blessing is truly ours until God has blessed someone else with it through us.

PHILLIPS BROOKS

33

It's Not So Easy to Forgive!

Bear with each other and forgive whatever grievances you may have against one another. Forgive as the Lord forgave you.
Colossians 3:13

Dear Jesus,

Do You get tired of me asking Your forgiveness? I can imagine You do, especially when I just say it as part of my daily prayers —a blanket request to cover any sin I've committed since the last time I prayed. I probably don't deserve Your forgiveness if I don't even bother to pinpoint any particular wrong!

I don't know why that suddenly struck me this morning, but it made me start thinking about something else I've been praying about. For some time now I've been asking You to forgive me for all the rotten things I did to _____ last year. (Reader: God and I know this person's name, but I'm sure all of us could fill in a name from our own experience.) And for the bad attitude I had toward her. How many times have I lamented about this? Am I making You a liar if I keep asking? I want to believe You've forgiven me, but I haven't forgotten about it.

35

I wonder about how much my ability to reach out in love to others has been hampered by not fully accepting Your forgiveness. If Paul would have condemned himself for killing Christians, he wouldn't have been an effective witness to others about Your love and forgiveness.

Maybe I'm not sure You've forgiven me because I haven't forgiven *her*—for the way she treated me! She never asked me to; so I never thought to do it. I think I need to forgive her so that I can accept Your forgiveness and forget all the ugliness of that relationship.

It might help to talk to someone else about the whole situation too. I've confessed it over and over again to You, but to erase it from my mind I may need to confess it to another friend.

I don't want to ignore guilt when I've done something wrong. But I don't want to punish myself with guilt either, especially when I know You can relieve me of this burden. Thank You for the grace You offer to me, Jesus. Teach me to accept the freedom it brings.

In Your grace,
Sandy

36

Life that ever needs forgiveness has for its first duty to forgive.

EDWARD GEORGE BULWER-LYTTON

37

Learning More About Love

Love the Lord your God with all your heart and with all your soul and with all your mind. This is the first and greatest commandment. And the second is like it: Love your neighbor as yourself.
                              Matthew 22:37–39

Dear Jesus,

On my way home from work today, my mind was skipping back and forth from past to present to future. Suddenly my mind said very distinctly, "Sandy, you're a neat person." I couldn't believe I just up and told myself that. It's *not* the kind of thing I usually go around saying!

Then I got to wondering, *Why don't I say it? Why don't I hear other people saying it about themselves?* I think I know why. I'm afraid that if anyone heard me they might disagree. Or they might be turned off by what seems to be vanity.

Maybe that's *not* the kind of thing we should say to other people, Jesus. But it does give me a warm feeling to say it to You tonight. And to know I believe it myself. I'm not always so convinced that I'm important. In fact, sometimes I'm sure I'm quite un-important.

I guess what it boils down to is prais-ing You. You're the One who gives me the opportunity to do neat things and the gifts to do them. And You're the one who helps me as I do them.

When I dislike myself, I'm really saying You're doing a lousy job. But You made me and I've chosen to live for You. If I don't accept myself, then I'm complaining about Your work and Your possessions! I'm saying I don't think You're doing as good a job as You could be.

Wow, I never thought about it like that before! I'm not going to run out and tell everyone I meet that I'm a neat person, but there are other ways to show that I like Sandy. I'm beginning to see that self-esteem isn't bad, and it's not the same as being conceited. Loving myself and working for You as Your child may be the highest thanks I can give You.

Thanks for the excitement of a new revelation and for helping me learn to love me. Keep speaking, Jesus!

Gratefully Yours,
Sandy

True humility is not an abject, groveling, self-despising spirit; it is but a right estimate of ourselves as God sees us.

TYRON EDWARDS

41

I'm Here, Jesus, But Where Are You?

If I go up to the heavens, you are there; if I make my bed in the depths, you are there. If I rise on the wings of the dawn, if I settle on the far side of the sea, even there your hand will guide me, your right hand will hold me fast.

Psalm 139:8–10

Dear Jesus,

I've designated this time to spend with You, Jesus, and now that I'm here, where are You? My head knows You're here, but I don't feel You. Right now that's important too.

Am I too much of an emotion-based believer? Sometimes I can almost feel Your arms around me. And then I can share that love with people I meet.

It's not always that grand and glorious, though, and right now is one of those other times. To tell You the truth, Jesus, I'd rather be writing to my friend Paul right now, because I know he'll write back. I want a concrete response from you, too.

Wow, that sounds selfish, doesn't it? But You know my emotions don't control my beliefs, Jesus. Thank You that faith doesn't have to depend on feelings.

Sometimes the undisciplined part of me takes over and I miss our quiet time together. You seem far away then, and it's not hard to know who is at fault. I'm the one who moved, and it's my job to get back on track.

This time, though, I know I've taken time to be with You every day. So I wonder, *Did You move?*

Even while I write that, Jesus, I know I'm only fooling myself. I've spent time with You all right—maybe fifteen minutes a day. But we haven't really been communicating. I've just been reading a few verses from the Bible and calling it meditation. I've been telling You to guide me in what I had already planned for the day. I've been calling this prayer. I've been sitting quietly and calling it listening for Your direction—when in fact my mind was going off in many directions.

Forgive me, Jesus. And help me to remember that I don't always need to *feel* Your closeness to know that You're always very near. Help me also to know when the distance between us is caused by my lack of commitment. Bring me back to You, Jesus.

Still struggling,
Sandy

Emotionalism never finds depths of truth, but depth of truth cannot be had apart from the full and free emotional response.

NELS F. S. FERRE

45

Moving Time

Do not conform any longer to the pattern of this world, but be transformed by the renewing of your mind. Then you will be able to test and approve what God's will is—his good, pleasing and perfect will.

Romans 12:2

Dear Jesus,

I've been thinking about the things I do with my time. Suddenly the choices I've made seem very narrow and unchallenging! Sure, every once in a while I do try something new. But before I start I want to be quite sure of doing a good job.

How can I ever expect to do anything out of the ordinary? It's not that I think I'll do anything that later generations will study in history class. No, I'm wondering if I'm living up to my potential. Basically, I'm just doing what comes naturally.

The most I ever stretch myself is when I strive to live up to others' expectations—expectations I'd have considered too high for myself! I'd hate to see myself if I hadn't been encouraged by special people all through my life, people who gave me the boost I needed to confront challenges. Without them I'd probably be like a smashed acorn—useless.

But isn't it true that often I put limits on myself? I hold myself back by listening only

47

to what society says a young person can do. I stay within the traditional roles for women—even though these are beginning to expand, thank goodness. The expectations of others can limit me, but they can also be challenges.

I want to begin a new chapter in my life, Jesus. I want to step out of my old patterns and try new things—things that I've never even dreamed about. I'm sure You want me to expand my horizons and not to limit Your call to what I'm used to doing.

This new thought brings some expectancy. If I open myself completely to You, You will use me in new ways. I've been satisfied doing so little! Shake me out of my complacency, Jesus. Help me realize my potential. Help me to be all that You know I can be!

Ready and rarin' to go,
Sandy

The woods would be very silent if no birds sang there except those who sang best.

JOHN JAMES AUDUBON

Change

*Jesus Christ is the same yesterday and today
and forever.*

Hebrews 13:8

Dear Jesus,

Change is a scary thing to think about—especially for someone who likes to be in control. Here I am, though, thinking about it anyway; so I may as well talk to You about it!

I'm thinking about how much change goes on all the time, Jesus. Even when I stay in one place, all kinds of change occurs—in my values, priorities, even in my plans for the evening or weekend! And change goes on in the world, and this affects me, too. Changes such as war and food shortages. All this makes me realize that You're the only part of my life that will never change.

I won't always be with the friends I have now. The security of today, of being with people I'm comfortable with and love, could change tomorrow. Then I think how complete the loss would be if I didn't have You, Jesus. Thank you for the assurance that You'll never move away!

I spent this Thanksgiving with a friend

51

whose father died a year ago. All the brothers and sisters and the grandchildren, with my friend's mother, celebrated Thanksgiving Day and the marriage of the youngest brother. We had a good time together, but the absence of their father and grandfather spoke loudly. Even though I had never met him, I found myself crying several times. I could see and feel the void his death had created.

I, too, will never know when I've seen someone for the last time. It's of infinite comfort to me that I have one Friend who will always be here. Thank You, Father, that I know You'll never die.

Friendships change too. That's scary, and it makes me want to control people. I want to make them love me forever. I know, though, it's only when I allow others to love me freely that it's truly love. Thank You, Jesus, that I can trust You to love me with an everlasting love.

Sometimes I wonder how anyone can cope with change if they don't have You as the stablizing factor in their life! How can anyone live without You, Jesus?

Thank You for being my hope in life— for being the Constant that enables me to deal with change.

Constantly Yours,
Sandy

52

*He who fears the LORD has a secure fortress,
and for his children it will be a refuge.*

PROVERBS 14:26

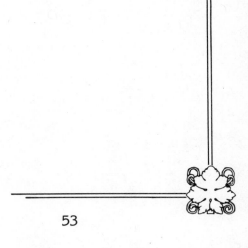

53

Part Two

I Search My Soul

I Want to Be Alone

Then, because so many people were coming and going that they did not even have a chance to eat, he said to [his disciples], "Come with me by yourselves to a quiet place and get some rest."

Mark 6:31

Dear Jesus,

When You lived here, did You ever get tired of smiling and being nice to everyone? Did You ever have to force Yourself to be friendly? Did you ever really not want to talk to anybody?

Well, I feel like that today. I wish I didn't, because it seems silly and immature. But I can't seem to overcome it. I'm not depressed or angry. I'd rather be alone and not have to decide how I feel every time someone asks, "How are you?" Do they really want to know?

I was determined not to let the January blahs set in. Last year January seemed so dull after the excitement of Thanksgiving, Christmas, and New Year's. Since I realized why I'd been hit so hard last year, I figured I could prevent it this year. I'm not doing too well, am I?

So what *is* wrong with me? Last night I went to choir practice, and I acted real happy. I pretended to be having a good time,

57

but laughing with everyone was about the last thing I felt like doing! I joined in so I wouldn't have to explain why I felt gloomy.

Thanks for listening to me again, Jesus. It helps to be able to share my feelings with You. You help me sort out what I'm feeling, and this helps me to understand what I'm thinking. This mood seems trite and insignificant, but when I let it build up inside, it starts controlling my actions. It's good to know You never think my problems are small or stupid. It helps a lot to admit that I'm not always overjoyed to be alive. And it's good to know it's OK if I don't feel like being friendly to everyone all the time.

Help me learn how to be myself, without taking either my joy or my sadness to the extreme. I want to be an enjoyable person to be with, but not by pretending to be somebody I'm not.

Your loving daughter,
Sandy

What would a man do if he were compelled to live always in the sultry heat of society, and could never better himself in cool solitude?

NATHANIEL HAWTHORNE

59

Single, Free,
and Happy
to Be . . . ?

*Now the Lord is the Spirit, and where the
Spirit of the Lord is, there is freedom.*
                    2 Corinthians 3:17

Dear Jesus,

I was thinking about my "single, free, and happy to be" pitch tonight—about the dreams I have of things I want to do alone or with others, and being glad that I'm free to do them. I can talk quite convincingly about the joys of being totally on my own, with no one to tie me down. And it's not just all talk. I really believe it and feel it.

Something about the independence of traveling, acting like I know what I'm doing, stirs up an excitement in me that happens only when I'm alone. I think about working in the mountains or in the city—but without making too long a commitment in case I hate it! Or maybe I'll live in another country.

Even if I never do any of these things, I'll cherish being able to go where I want to go, moving on to a new challenge when I want to, and staying there as long as I like. I want to explore different places, people, lifestyles, and jobs to determine how I can best be used as Your servant. I know I have a lot to learn about myself and about loving and trusting You completely before I can commit myself to anyone else for the rest of my life.

I love meeting lots of different people, too—and being able to choose how to use my time and who my friends are. I like being alone to play the piano, walk in the rain, roll down a hill, eat breakfast at noon—or not eat if I feel like being hungry. I love making last-minute decisions—like stopping to see friends on my way home for Christmas. And responsibilities, such as deciding how to use my money, planning a worship service, or planning my time, can be challenging and fulfilling.

It's exhilarating for me to accomplish something and know that I did a good job without anyone's help—except Yours of course. I don't want to lose sight of my dependence on You in my exploration of independence.

I'm still young and I want to enjoy to the fullest my singleness and the freedom it brings. If I'm going to be married someday, please don't let me meet him for a while yet, OK?

Joyfully,
Sandy

Look well into thyself; there is a source of strength which will always spring up if thou wilt always look there.

MARCUS ANTONIUS

63

Why Do I Fear?

When I am afraid, I will trust in you. In God,
whose word I praise, in God I trust.
Psalm 56:3–4

Dear Jesus,

I've got a tightness in my stomach that feels like it'll keep gnawing at me until it infects every part of my body. If You promise not to tell anyone, Jesus, I'll tell You what I think it is. I think it's fear.

It's taken me a long time to diagnose, because there's nothing that's really scaring me. It's more like a knot that keeps getting tighter. I don't notice it when I'm having a good time, but it returns when I'm in bed at night or relaxing. It's not just being alone either. It's there when I'm with other people.

I noticed it again this morning while I was reading the newspaper. I shouldn't read it during breakfast. It ruins my favorite meal every time!

Among the top news stories were the account of a child who was raped, the never-ending controversy over who should supply whom with military weapons, the next "case" to die in the electric chair, and on and on.

Most of these stories don't seem real,

but they're extremely real to those whose lives are touched. This makes me afraid that I can never really be secure. I've always had enough to eat, a place to sleep, clothes to wear, and a family who cares about me. But everyone isn't that fortunate, and I may not always be either. It scares me even to think about this!

It would be no comfort if there were others starving with me or being bombed or in prison with me. These would be lonely and terrifying experiences if a person was alone or with others. Is that the kind of loneliness You felt in death, Jesus? I can't imagine Your agony.

I guess that makes being Your friend unique. You understand my fears from Your own experience. It's been good for me to admit my fears to myself and to You, Jesus. I know if I feel alone, it's not because You've left me. It's because I'm not recognizing Your presence amidst the world's instability.

Holding on to Your hand,
Sandy

The miserable have no other medicine but only hope: I've hope to live, and am prepar'd to die.

WILLIAM SHAKESPEARE

My Friends and I

I have called you friends, for everything that I learned from my Father I have made known to you.

John 15:15

Dear Jesus,

I miss CJ so much today I can actually feel the ache—as if my heart's sore from doing too many sit-ups! I know I have lots of other friends I could be with and who are important to me, but CJ meets my needs in ways that no one else can. At least no one has yet, and it's been several months since she left.

I'm not thinking of anything that I couldn't write her in a letter. I just want to drop in at her place. I'd like to tell her how my day's going and hear how she is. And maybe we'd go for a bike ride or eat lunch in the park. Or we could play our guitars and sing on the back porch.

Someone once told me that everyone should have at least twenty good friends, and I'm starting to see the wisdom of that advice. These don't have to be the kind of people you go to with a problem at any time, but each one of my friends can relate to a different need in me.

69

I never thought of myself as a complex person, but I guess that's how You made us. That means, too, that I can never expect one person to meet all my needs. So maybe it's healthy to miss CJ today. Maybe the part of her that became a part of me can't be replaced by anyone else.

I know this could leave me feeling fragmented, Jesus—if I didn't have Your friendship. You know every part of me, even better than I do, and You hold all these parts together. No wonder people who don't know You feel lost! Most of them probably have friends, but without Someone who is greater holding all their relationships together and filling in the gaps, friends aren't as meaningful as they could be.

Jesus, there is a beauty in missing CJ. I know it means no one can replace her. Thank You, most of all, for being the friend who knows every part of me.

With love and adoration,
Sandy

A true friend is the gift of God, and he only who made hearts can unite them.

ROBERT SOUTH

71

Up From Failure

My grace is sufficient for you, for my power is made perfect in weakness.

2 Corinthians 12:9

Dear Jesus,

I was looking at the brittle shell of a locust this afternoon and wishing I could do what it had done. I wish I could just crawl out of this old self and hop away. I'd love to forget all the things that keep me bound to who I am now. I don't know who I'd rather be, but I fall so short of being the person I know I could be—and that You want me to be—that I get discouraged.

Does that sound brash, Jesus? That's my reaction to how I've been feeling all week. It's as if I can't do anything right, and the harder I try the more I fail. I really don't think You give up on me that easily, though, so why am I ready to give up? I suppose it's normal to hate failure, but I can't be perfect no matter how hard I try. So what can I do with that ugly part of me?

Being able to admit this to You, Jesus, and knowing You love me and accept me anyway, helps me to feel a little better about myself. Everyone fails. The difference is in

73

how I react to it. Ignoring it keeps me from learning anything. If I can get it through my head that weakness isn't totally worthless, then I can grow from the lessons it teaches me.

Even though You didn't fail, there are many examples of failure in Your followers. Peter once failed to own Your friendship. Judas failed to see Your eternal Lordship. They chose their own fate in their response to their mistakes. You continued to give both of them Your love. The difference is that Judas let himself be crushed by his wrong and Peter renewed his efforts to live for You.

I guess I don't want to run away from who I am after all, Jesus. I'd rather use the things I've learned from my failure to grow. Thank You for accepting me while working with me at improvement. Keep my failure from being devastating.

Striving on,
Sandy

There is no failure so great that a Christian cannot rise from it, there is no defeat so final that he cannot convert it into a victory.

HELEN C. WHITE

75

Anger: Right or Wrong?

In your anger do not sin.

Ephesians 4:26

Dear Jesus,

I'm still trying to recuperate from the shock of seeing Titus so angry today. I kept expecting him to come to his senses and apologize. But when it was over, he seemed pleased with himself!

I can understand his anger. I was angry too when the waitress refused to serve that black woman. The difference between Titus and me was that I just let my anger boil inside and Titus expressed his in a phone call to the manager.

The reason I was so surprised at his reaction is that I've seen him respond with love when people abused him. Just like we're taught in Sunday School! But this time Titus wasn't being discriminated against. A powerless person was being hurt. Then, through his controlled but powerful anger, he acted.

Was that wrong, Jesus? I can hardly believe it was, because I see Titus working so faithfully to be in Your will and purpose. I remember, too, that You were angry when

You found people misusing Your house of worship.

So why was I so surprised? I've somehow gotten the impression that it's wrong to be angry, or at least to show it. I've often seen the negative effects of anger, but maybe I haven't seen enough healthy anger —the kind You had toward injustice. Maybe I don't care enough to be angry! Or maybe I'm afraid people won't like me as much if they see that side of me.

I can tell I have a lot to learn about anger, Jesus. My first step is probably to admit that it's real. Then I can learn positive ways to channel it. I'm beginning to see how today's incident can help me. It's making me look at myself and also at how You handled anger. What a great example You are for me, Jesus. Help me to keep understanding Your example more and more.

Love,
Sandy

Reason opposes evil the more effectively when anger ministers at her side.

POPE ST. GREGORY THE GREAT

79

Am I Oversensitive?

Worship the Lord your God, and serve him only.

Matthew 4:10

Dear Jesus,

Why do I let what other people say control my feelings? I get angry at myself for being so wishy-washy, but how can I learn to react differently?

We both know how much I admire _____, but that's no reason to let her opinion of me—or my work—regulate how I think. I've let things she's said ruin my whole day! It works the other way too. If she compliments me, it can brighten my day.

It feels good to be encouraged by a compliment, but my reaction to criticism makes me stop and think. Letting myself be controlled like that is bad whether the result is happiness or unhappiness. Is sensitivity always good, or can we be oversensitive?

She didn't say anything mean to me today. She just asked me why I hadn't gone to the meeting last night. But I got the impression she thought I should have been there. I felt awful and wished I would have gone, just to have her approval. Now I wish I

81

would have decided for myself, and then felt good about my decision no matter what she thought.

I'm starting to see the need for a distinct line between accommodating others and believing in myself. I musn't let myself be swayed too much by what others think or say. Jesus, help me find the right balance between sensitivity and oversensitivity. I don't want to offend anyone, but I also want to think and act according to who I know myself to be. Help me to keep discovering who I am and to be proud of what we will do with that together. Thanks for Your patience with me, Jesus.

Eternally Yours,
Sandy

An humble knowledge of thyself is a surer way to God than a deep search after learning.

THOMAS À KEMPIS

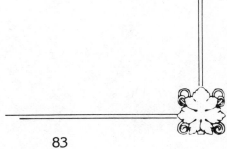

83

Would Anyone Miss Me?

When I consider your heavens, the work of your fingers, the moon and the stars, which you have set in place, what is man that you are mindful of him, the son of man that you care for him?

Psalm 8:3–4

Dear Jesus,

I was just looking up at the huge sky, pierced with millions of glittering stars. And I realized once again how secure I am in Your universe. I was feeling very close to You—imagining that You had created all the stars and planets just for me.

Then I thought about how many other people—in many other lands—are watching those same stars, and suddenly I felt tiny and insignificant. The earth is such a small part of Your creation! What's the difference if we blow ourselves apart? Will it be just one less sparkle to light tonight's blackness?

And what about here on earth? With the population increasing by 160,000 people each day, my life doesn't seem very important. My friends and family will cry when I die, but what difference will it really make? Life will go on, and two more will be born to take my place.

What does it matter whether or not I come home exhausted from helping people?

Poor people will survive without the money I give to relief agencies. Next Sunday's worship service would happen even if I hadn't just spent half a day planning it.

In comparison to the great people of history, or a lot of my friends, I dabble in many areas rather than do anything well.

But Jesus, the fact that I'm writing to You proves that I know You care. What would I do without You? How do people who don't know You and Your reassuring friendship maintain a sense of worth or significance?

It's good to be reminded again that I'm not indispensable. The world could get along without me. My task is to be responsible with the time and gifts You've given me. Each person I touch is a gift from You. Thank You that belonging to You gives me significance, Jesus. Thanks, too, for the knowledge that I can never be replaced.

In You,
Sandy

So long as men and women believed themselves to be responsible beings, called to choose, and accountable to God for their choices, life might be tragic, but it was not trivial.

SIDNEY CAVE

87

Please Love Me

God has said, "Never will I leave you; never will I forsake you." So we say with confidence, "The Lord is my helper; I will not be afraid."

Hebrews 13:5–6

Dear Jesus,

Will I ever be satisfied with myself? Will I ever totally accept who I am and who I'm not? And are You wondering the same thing, Jesus?

I feel so wishy-washy. It wasn't too long ago that I was enthusiastic about being independent and single, but I'm not so sure tonight. Part of me wants to be held and be told that I'm somebody special. I know I'm special to You, Jesus, and possibly to a lot of other people too. But I want another *person* to tell me I'm special. Someone who can share more of love than just words.

Part of me wants to tell someone about the rabbit I saw on the road tonight—half squished and half squirming—and for that someone to care about the rabbit and to care that I care. It would just be nice having someone sitting in another chair near me.

Part of me wants to know that no matter what happens in the world, I won't be alone. Or if I want to be alone, it's nice to know that someone will be waiting when I return.

But is sharing a special love with one other person and having the security of that commitment any more secure than life itself? It's risky to love because you hurt all the more if something happens to that love.

Tonight I feel willing to take that risk. I have a lot of love to give, and I want to be loved in a special way.

Putting these feelings into words and saying them to You, Jesus, gives me much comfort. Knowing You means that I have the answer I'm searching for within myself. Even when I want to be loved by a fellow human being, I know that You love and care for me in ways I'll never comprehend.

Thanks for being patient with me. I need to remember to keep coming to You. It's great to know You're always here—watching, waiting, and wanting to love me, just as I am.

Resting in Your loving care,
Sandy

There is not one life which the Life-giver ever loses out of His sight: not one which sins so that He casts it away: not one which is not so near to Him that whatever touches it touches Him with sorrow or with joy.

PHILLIPS BROOKS

Fed Up!

Do not worry about your life, what you will eat or drink; or about your body, what you will wear. Is not life more important than food, and the body more important than clothes?

Matthew 6:25

Dear Jesus,

I'm so sick of myself! And I'm sure You're sick of me too. I know I shouldn't eat so much, and then I go and do it anyway. It's bad enough I eat junk food that doesn't do anything except make me fat, but then I keep eating the stuff even though I'm full! I know it's a sin to eat more than I need, especially when so many people in this world are starving. How can I keep eating as if I don't even care?

It's not something I can talk to anyone else about either. They'd just tell me to quit eating. I know that's what I *should* do, and it's what I *want* to do, but it's not that easy.

Most people have it all figured out—they eat too much when they're depressed. Or when they're worried. Or when they're happy. I have myself figured out too. I eat too much all the time!

I do have control sometimes, though. And I *can* lose weight. I always feel better about myself at these times, but as soon as I

93

ease up, I pig out and the weight goes right back on. I could exercise more, but isn't that, too, a luxury if I'm doing it just because I've eaten too much?

I'm ashamed to have to come to You like this, Jesus, but I know You won't love me any less. In fact, more than anyone, I know You accept me just like I am, all the while supporting my desire to change. Thanks for that.

I'm angry at myself right now, but I don't feel hopeless. I need to let this anger move me to choose different eating habits. I also need Your help in this self-control project, Jesus. Keep reminding me that overeating is a sin and that having good eating patterns will have benefit throughout my life—not just while I'm losing ten pounds!

Fed up,
Sandy

Self-discipline never means giving up anything—for giving up is a loss. Our Lord did not ask us to give up the things of earth, but to exchange them for better things.

FULTON J. SHEEN

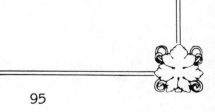

95

Part Three

I Give My Heart

Where'd the Day Go?

Encourage the timid, help the weak, be patient with everyone.

1 Thessalonians 5:14

Dear Jesus,

Another day's almost gone, and I didn't get a thing done! We both know that can't be true, because I've been busy all day. But when I don't do the things I plan, I feel like I've wasted the whole day.

As usual, I started out making a list of everything I wanted to do today. I was thinking how great it was to have a free Saturday—a whole day to myself! So why didn't it stay that way?

I wanted to make bread, but I didn't have the right kind of flour. I wanted to wash clothes, but the washer was already being used. I wanted to clean the house, but I didn't feel like cleaning up everyone else's junk first.

I stayed in the house all day waiting for Mary Ellen to call, but she never did. I wanted to go for a walk because it was a beautiful day, but I never got a chance until after dark—and then it started raining!

I did get at least five other phone calls,

99

though, and Chris came over for two hours.

As I write all this to You now, Jesus, it must sound silly. I do like to have friends over, and usually I love to walk in the rain. I get so uptight, though, when my schedule gets messed up. Looking back now, I realize it wasn't so terrible. In fact, today probably would have been even better than the day I'd planned if I'd have relaxed and welcomed the surprises.

Why is it so hard to live what I believe —that people are more important than things? I thought I was too busy to ask Chris to stay for supper. When Beth called, she might have been lonely, but I was in too much of a hurry to find out.

Why am I in such a hurry? Forgive me, Jesus. Slow me down. Help me to relax and to be more sensitive to my friends, Your children. They may need me more than I need to maintain a schedule. Help me to follow Your example of giving people top priority.

Yours for the training,
Sandy

If you are losing your leisure, look out; you may be losing your soul.

LOGAN PEARSALL SMITH

101

More Than My Share

Jesus said to his disciples, "I tell you the truth, it is hard for a rich man to enter the kingdom of heaven."

Matthew 19:23

Dear Jesus,

"What we have is ours only because God has given it to us." That's what the preacher said, and I know it's true. But sometimes I feel like the prodigal son. He took "his" inheritance, which was only his because his father gave it to him, and went off to spend it.

That son has always seemed selfish to me, but the more possessions I have, the more I see selfishness in myself. It scares me, Jesus!

For many people in this world, walking is their only means of transportation. How would I explain to them that I own both a bicycle and a car? How could I tell a person who feels fortunate to have one or two outfits that I have a closet full of clothes? Can I "afford" to eat at nice restaurants, when many in the world don't know what it is to eat three meals in one day?

Jesus, have You decided to bless me more because You love me more? I know

103

that's not true! But still I find ways to rationalize this inequality.

One way I do this is to compare myself to people who have more than I. And before I know it, I'm forgetting about those who are fortunate. My wealth always returns to haunt me, though. And this is good, because it probably means I haven't become totally calloused.

I'm rich in many other ways, too. In education, health, experience, future opportunities. I'm rich in love, freedom, and peace.

If all these gifts really are from You, Jesus, and You're allowing me to borrow them for a while, I have a tremendous responsibility to use them well! It leaves no room for selfishness, for thinking I need to control everything I own. I need to listen to what You tell me I need rather than to what those around me would have me think.

Jesus, keep me from feeling so guilty about my richness that I don't enjoy life's goodness. But also keep me from becoming so content with luxuries that I forget those less fortunate than myself.

Keep me growing,
Sandy

Genuine Christianity teaches men not so much how to make and save riches as to how to get rid of them with the greatest possible advantage of their eternal salvation.

IGNATIUS SMITH

Behind Bars

The Spirit of the Lord is on me, . . . He has sent me to proclaim freedom for the prisoners and recovery of sight for the blind, to release the oppressed, to proclaim the year of the Lord's favor.

Luke 4:18–19

Dear Jesus,

How can it be? How can one person have so much power over another?

I've passed by that building every time I've gone downtown, but before today I've never stopped to think about the people inside. People who can't go shopping when they want to, or see the people they want to see, or eat what they want to eat!

I keep reliving those first few moments. I cringed as the huge iron door locked behind me. I was alone with the echo of the guard's voice. He said he'd be back in an hour. There was only one way to go—straight down that dark narrow hall. At the end of that corridor I saw Judy, peering through the bars of her cell.

Jesus, how do You feel when we don't listen to Your children who are locked up in prison? This is only a small part of our country's prison system, but I hope I'll never forget it. I saw a very lonely woman, who desperately wants to be with her child. I saw

107

evidence of talents that are being wasted. Those bars imprisoned me too—they prevented me from giving her even a consoling hug.

I'm caught between my anger and my happiness at being able to visit tonight. That gigantic key, those bars, Judy's scared, hollow face, each of these is permanently imprinted in my memory. Prisoners are no longer mere statistics, because now I know one of them. I know Judy as a friend. Someone who hurts, laughs, cries, and loves. Someone who wants to be listened to, just like me. Jesus, I can't help but think You hate the way prisons control people.

I feel some guilt now, too, because I so seldom say or do anything about the oppression of Judy and others. Forgive me, Jesus. Help me never to stop being angry at injustice. Keep me from becoming calloused to the pain of Your children. As much as I hated being in that jail tonight, I know—already now—that there was a purpose. Thank You for letting me meet Judy and help me to do this again.

Your indignant servant,
Sandy

While there is a lower class I am in it, while there is a criminal element I am of it, while there is a soul in prison I am not free.

EUGENE DEBS

There's More to Friendship Than Fun!

Now that you have purified yourselves by obeying the truth so that you have sincere love for your brothers, love one another deeply, from the heart.

1 Peter 1:22

Dear Jesus,

I thought the personal awareness group I joined was going to be fun. Maybe it will be, but I see a threatening side to it too. Last night, the leader gave us an assignment. We're to think of four people who know us well, and ask each of them to write down one good thing about us.

My first reaction was that I don't want to put my friends on the spot. Then I decided I'd hide behind the fact that it's an assignment. The jolt came when I began to think about who I'd ask. I realized I don't know four people here who know me well enough to do it!

I spend a lot of time with people, and I've always felt very blessed to have a good number of friends. But is it possible to have too many friends, Jesus? Do I spread myself too thin and end up with too few quality relationships?

When You lived on earth Your life touched many people. But You also had a core group, Your disciples. I guess after three years with the same twelve people, Your group became an important means of support for each one of you. In the Bible the emphasis is often on what the disciples learned from You, but for that to happen, they had to know You.

Maybe I should have fewer friends and put my energy into supporting that smaller group. It's fun to know lots of people, but I can also see the rewards of having several close friends—people you're accountable to.

It's scary to face the fact that I'm far away from the people I've always called my friends, but it also feels like a nudge toward more meaning in my most important relationships.

Keep pushing me, Jesus. I'm sure I'll come to know You better through this new experience!

Ever-wondering, ever-learning,
Sandy

True happiness consists not in the multitude of friends, but in their worth and choice.

BEN JONSON

113

Glenn

And I heard a loud voice from the throne saying, . . . "There will be no more death or mourning or crying or pain, for the old order of things has passed away."
Revelation 21:3-4

Dear Jesus,

I feel sad tonight. It's not a sadness I can explain to anyone, because no one else knows how much Glenn meant to me. I'm glad You do, Jesus. I need to talk to You alone, because I don't want to be cheered up. I know You'll let me be sad.

I didn't expect this afternoon to be any different than any of the other Thursday afternoons I've spent visiting Glenn at the nursing home. It's been three years since I first met him and adopted him as a special friend.

I don't know if he ever understood why I came, but it wasn't long before he was expecting me each week. I could always tell, because he started saving apples for me. I couldn't eat them because sometimes they were rotten and they *always* carried the medicine smell of his room. But I still cherished that gift.

The first year we met, Glenn told me lots of stories about his childhood. And we

115

laughed together a lot. The next year both his memory and his eyesight began to dim; so he would ask me to read newspaper articles to him—especially the obituaries! I don't think he could hear much of what I said, but I know he liked having me near.

This past year, Glenn seemed to be in a world of his own. He could hardly see or hear, and he was barely strong enough to shift his long body in his bed. I reached out to bridge the gap by holding his hand while we both sat silent, sometimes for an hour or more. He would gently squeeze my hand and whisper thanks as I stood to leave. Sometimes he held on, begging me not to go. Sometimes his good-byes were quiet tears.

But today the room was empty, and there weren't any apples in his window. I thought perhaps they had moved him to a different room. But when I asked the nurse, her face told me that Glenn had moved for the last time.

In Your comfort,
Sandy

Those who live in the Lord never see each other for the last time.

GERMAN MOTTO

117

We Can't All Help the Indians!

For we are God's workmanship, created in Christ Jesus to do good works, which God prepared in advance for us to do.

Ephesians 2:10

Dear Jesus,

Thanks for the feeling of freedom that came over me this afternoon. I hardly knew what I was doing! That can be bad, I know, but today it worked out better than if I had planned it. I don't know why I think of some people as being so great they'd never talk to an ordinary person like me. Especially when they're a brother or sister in Your family.

I've admired Lawrence Hart ever since I read his article about the injustices that American Indians suffer. He knows, because he's a Cheyenne chief. Two pages of his writing hit harder at my lack of caring and my inaction than ten sermons put together!

I was at a conference today. When I looked across the room and saw "Lawrence Hart" on his name tag, all the guilt I feel about the way we've oppressed the American Indian and the awe I've felt for this man came flooding over me. I still don't know how we started talking, but I felt relaxed and comfortable with him almost immediately.

119

I told this man how much I've been influenced by his writings, and his response to me was overwhelming. He said he doesn't want me to feel guilty if helping in the struggle of the American Indian isn't a top priority in my life. He helped me to see that they need the concern and energetic work of Your people, but many other people do too. If I try to work at every injustice I hear about, I won't be effective in any of them.

That was good for me to hear, Jesus. It's best to choose one or two areas where I have knowledge, skill, and interest and help alleviate pain and injustice for these people. This is better than spreading myself so thin that I don't do anything well. It's exciting to be involved in lots of things, but not if it means I can't give my best to any of them.

Lead me in discovering my interests and gifts, Jesus. Help me to do my best without feeling guilty about those I can't help. Help me, also, to remember that I'm only a worker for You and that obedience to Your will is more important than being Superwoman.

Submissively,
Sandy

*Nothing is really lost by a life of sacrifice;
everything is lost by failure to obey God's call.*

HENRY PARRY LIDDON

On Confessing

Love is patient, love is kind.... It keeps no record of wrongs.

1 Corinthians 13:4–5

Dear Jesus,

I'm confused about a letter I received today. It was from a girl I knew when I lived in Pennsylvania. She said she's felt bitter toward me for some time and wants to ask my forgiveness.

I was totally shocked! I didn't know her well, and certainly don't know why she didn't like me. The part that puzzles me most is why she told me any of this. She's telling me she wants me to know and at the same time she wants me to forget! Is this her way of getting back at me?

I'm sorry, Jesus. I know this is being judgmental. Maybe this is the only way she can find release. Or maybe this is how she understands your words about Christians confessing their sins to one another. It's making me think about how I handle similar situations. I talk with a person about a problem we're having only when *both* of us agrees there *is* a problem. If we think it's something we need to settle—so that we can

123

forgive each other—then it seems appropriate to talk it out.

If I'm the only one with the hang-up, though, it seems like You and I can settle it alone, Jesus. If I share my struggle with the other person, I'd be getting rid of the problem for myself. But this would be the beginning of a problem for the other person! That doesn't seem fair. The only way I could justify that would be to know for certain that such a confession will help the person I've sinned against. Maybe if this girl had told me the part I played in causing her bitter feelings, I could use this to improve my interaction with others.

It sure helps to blow off steam to You, Jesus. My anger at this letter is losing power already. It's helped me think about how I should handle problems I have with another person, and when I should ask for the other person's forgiveness.

I want to be careful about confessing when it's detrimental to the other person, Jesus. I also want to stay open to changes You want me to make.

I love You,
Sandy

What is repentance but a kind of leave-taking, looking backward indeed, but yet in such a way as precisely to quicken the steps toward that which lies before.

SÖREN KIERKEGAARD

125

Some Things Are Best Left Unsaid

Do not let any unwholesome talk come out of your mouths, but only what is helpful for building others up according to their needs, that it may benefit those who listen.
Ephesians 4:29

Dear Jesus,

I don't feel good at all about how I treated one of the guys at the camp-out last weekend. I should probably talk to him about it, but I need to talk with You first. I need to straighten out in my own mind what my motives and reasons were.

I don't know him well, but something about his manner was repulsive to me from the start. That's a terrible thing to say, Jesus, but it's true. He's so conceited, and he tries to be funny—which he isn't. I don't usually let people bug me like that, but you don't have the option of ignoring someone at a camp-out!

I responded by making cutting remarks in the form of jokes. He was constantly saying and doing such stupid things! He and everyone else laughed at the slams, but they probably didn't realize that this was my way of releasing my tense feelings. I guess I didn't realize it fully either—until Brian asked me why I hated him so much. And he wasn't laughing any more.

I felt awful, Jesus. He saw right through my "jokes." I'm wondering how much I've done that with other people. How much of my joking is a cover for anger or other feelings? It's hard for me to confront people, and I like to laugh. So joking is a natural outlet for my angry feelings. But I guess it can turn into malicious teasing. I didn't think about it in that way, though, until Brian called my attention to it.

I don't like that part of me, Jesus, but it happens so fast. I guess I've been doing it for so long that it happens before I know it. I'll have to make a conscious effort to break the habit.

Jesus, help me say things that build up rather than tear down. I don't want to lose the spontaneity of laughter, but I need to limit it to what is good for everyone involved. Guide me in judging that and acting on it.

With love,
Sandy

What you keep by you, you may change and mend; but words, once spoken, can never be recalled.

ROSCOMMON

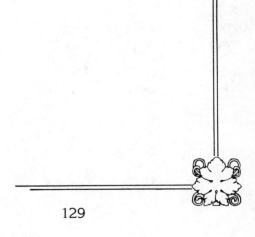

129

Making the First Move

[*Love*] *always protects, always trusts, always hopes, always perseveres.*

1 Corinthians 13:7

Dear Jesus,

I keep seeing that troubled face in my mind's eye! Today Ruth Ann told me _____ had a mental breakdown last month and is constantly battling depression. So this answered some of my questions, but I'm still baffled.

She wasn't a close friend of mine, but I always figured she wanted it that way. She's older than I, and she always seemed so self-confident! I thought she neither wanted nor needed my friendship.

Realizing what was inside of her all that time blows my mind! I completely misread her cries for love. I let her snobbish front scare me away from looking deeper—to the part that hated herself and wanted to know she's a worthwhile person.

How often do I look only on the surface, Jesus? I completely misjudged her. How many others have I overlooked who have needed me? How often have I let insensitivity, quick judgment, or selfishness control how I see others?

131

It scares me, Jesus, because it's so contrary to who You were and who You want me to be. You didn't let anyone scare You away from loving them. I'll bet You felt like it sometimes, though, didn't You?

It's a lot easier when people let you know they're hurting, but I guess that's too risky for an insecure person. I need to start looking for ways I can reach out to people who need love—even when they act as if they don't.

Jesus, give me the courage to step out of my own worries about not being accepted and initiate friendships. The people who most want and need friends are probably the least likely to make the first move. Help me to see each person as part of the family of God. And help all of us to realize that we need each other.

Looking to You and others,
Sandy

The greatest thing a man can do for his heavenly Father is to be kind to some of His other children.

HENRY DRUMMOND

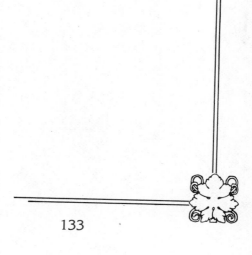

133

Don't Keep It Inside!

Name _Nancy Croyle_

Address _Goshen College_

Phone _533-3161_   Date _10/31/82_

Age (X)under 20 ( )21–30 ( )31–50 ( )over 50

( ) New in the area
( ) New address or phone
(X) College student
( ) Illness in the home
( ) Need transportation
(X) Visiting, guest of _Tami Goss_

Interested in discussing:
( ) Church Membership
( ) Sunday School
( ) Home Fellowships
( ) The Christian Faith
( ) Would like an appointment with a pastor

Names and ages of children _Oh, I'm an_
only child, thank you.
_____

PLEASANT VIEW MENNONITE CHURCH
58529 CR 23   (219) 533-2872
Goshen, IN 46526

We welcome you to participate with us as we worship the Lord Jesus Christ. It is our desire that you experience the love of Christ among us as we fellowship together.

To help us learn to know you better, please fill out this card and place it in the offering plate.

Thank you.

*Carry each other's burdens, and in this way
you will fulfill the law of Christ.*
                              Galatians 6:2

Dear Jesus,

It's been almost eight months now since I joined one of the small groups at church. But I didn't realize until last night how much of my life I've kept hidden from them. I don't think I did it on purpose. With everyone else having so many problems, mine didn't seem all that important.

That's probably why I haven't told them about the hard time I've been having at work. By the time I'd get to the meeting each week, work seemed far away. No one ever asked me how it was going; so I assumed they didn't care.

Now I know why my folks said, "Never assume anything." By last night, I'd had all the tension I could stand. Sharing with the group wasn't a matter of trust, it was a necessity! Otherwise I'd have fallen apart! I've been talking to You about it for a long time, Jesus, but suddenly I realized it was too big to keep inside.

I can't believe the way they responded!

Everyone listened more intently than I ever dreamed possible. Nancy suggested the group pray for me. And then I started crying—with joy this time! After the meeting Polly and Charles gave me a great big hug and said they'd be praying for me. Carolyn asked me to have lunch with her tomorrow, and Ginger told me to come over any time I wanted someone to talk to. Today, I got a note from Jim, assuring me of his thoughts and prayers, and Nora called to see how I'm doing.

I've been overwhelmed, Jesus. I know You want me to share my life with my spiritual brothers and sisters. Why am I so slow to let them know when I'm hurting? It's risky, but the rewards are greater than I ever imagined. I feel a renewed determination to go back to work and make the best of it. Now that I have people supporting me, I feel my desire to provide that love to others increasing. Maybe best of all, Jesus, I'm sure you're pleased to see Christians building each other up for Your kingdom!

Thank You so much,
Sandy

When love is real love, when people's souls go out to their beloved, when they lose their hearts to them, when they act in the unselfish way..., a miracle is produced.

ERNEST DIMNET

137